I0500301

Stock Investing

The Ultimate Beginner's Guide to Investing in the Stock Market Easily and Successfully

Table of Contents

Introduction

Congratulations on purchasing this book and thank you for doing so.

The following chapters will teach you everything that you need to know about investing in stocks.

Chapter 1 discusses the basics, so that you will have a better understanding of the stock market and how you can make money with it.

Chapter 2 talks about opening an investment account, so you can begin investing in stocks. It also shows the standards to look for when choosing a stockbroker.

Chapter 3 teaches the different strategies that you can use when you invest in stocks.

Chapter 4 lays down the best practices or keys to success that can significantly increase your chances of success.

Chapter 5 talks about the common mistakes that beginners make, as well as how you can avoid them.

Chapter 6 offers a guide on how you can get started and make your first investment in stocks.

Chapter 7 talks about the other things that you will encounter when you engage in the stock market, such as investing in penny stocks and options trading, among others.

There are plenty of books on this subject on the market, thanks again for choosing this one! Every effort was made to ensure it is full of as much useful information as possible. Please enjoy!

Chapter 1
The Basics

Investing your money in stocks is the best way to make money work for you. This is one of the reasons why so many people are interested in the stock market. This is also an effective way to achieve financial freedom.

Stock vs. stock market

A stock or share of stock represents ownership of a company. Corporations have multiple shares, and these shares are owned by different people. These are also the shares that you buy and sell in the stock market. The stock market simply refers to a place where people can buy and sell stocks.

There are many kinds of stocks, but when you hear investors talk about stocks, they usually refer to common stocks. These are the stocks commonly traded in the stock market.

It is worth noting that not all corporations can be found in the stock market. As a rule, to be listed in the stock market, the corporation must be a publicly-listed company. A publicly-listed company simply refers to a business that offers its stocks to the public. This is usually done in order to finance the operations of the company.

How to make money in the stock market

When you purchase stocks, or more specifically, common shares of a company, you get to buy ownership of a company.

Therefore, you also make money just like the business owners themselves. Hence, you also earn dividends and capital gains.

Dividends refer to the share of earnings of an investor in the company. They are normally declared by the board of directors of a company and are passed on to the holders of stocks. You might be wondering then why a company would declare dividends. The reason is that the board of directors themselves are also shareholders of the company, and by declaring dividends, they also earn. Also, in some states, there are laws preventing over-holding of dividends.

Capital gains or capital appreciation is the usual way by which an investor makes money. This means that the value of the stocks that you own had increased than that time when you bought them. For example, if you bought some stocks at the $10 per stock six months ago, and their value now is $20 per stock, then you have capital gains of 100%.

How much money can you make (or lose)?

The amount of money that you can make or lose by investing in stocks mainly depends on your willingness to learn, as well as how disciplined you are. Like any other investment or business, there are risks involved when you invest in stocks. For one, the stock market is inherently risky because it is difficult to predict the behavior of the market. There are also many factors that affect the prices of stocks, such as the economy, consumer behavior, government, competition, and others. There are also investors who lose their money due to ignorance. These are the people who do not take the time and effort to research and analyze the market.

Despite the risks involved, many people still invest their money in the stock market. The reason is that the stock market can be profitable if you have the right knowledge and the willingness to learn. Needless to say, being a successful investor also requires continuous practice.

A good thing about investing in stocks is that there is no limit as to how high you can earn. If you get lucky and pick really good stocks, you can even triple your investment within a year.

Is it difficult to make an investment?

Thanks to technology, you can now invest in the stock market from the comfort of your home. You simply have to open an account with an online broker, and you can start buying and selling stocks with just a few clicks of a mouse. This will be discussed in detail later on in this book.

Making an investment is easy. You can spend even just a few minutes a week. However, if you are serious about being a successful investor and would like to see a regular stream of profits flowing into your account, then you should know that continuous success in the stock market requires time, serious efforts, research and analysis, patience, and practice.

Investing in stocks vs. gambling

Since the stock market is hard to predict, some people think that investing in stocks is the same as gambling. So, is stock investing gambling? The answer to this question depends on your approach. If you make your investment simply based on pure luck or mere guesswork, then it is fair to say that you are gambling. However, if you spend serious effort and time in analyzing the factors that affect the behavior of the stock market, if you consider every stock that you buy or share as an investment decision, then you are investing and not just gambling.

The problem with approaching stock investing just as a form of gambling is that you cannot expect to have regular profits. In fact, based on how the stock market is designed, there is even a higher probability for you to lose all your investment money. If you are really serious about making money by investing in stocks, then you should treat it as a business or as a professional career.

Investing vs. trading

There is really no difference between investing in and trading stocks. But, for the word geeks out there, trading refers to a more active activity, since you can make multiple trades within a single day. Hence, there are day traders, which refer to people who trade stocks with a trading duration limited to one trading day. This means that they open their positions during the day and close out all their positions every evening. Investing entails a less active approach whereby you do not close your positions right away. You can wait for weeks, months, and even years before selling our stocks. While trading involves a short duration, investing involves holding on to your stocks for a longer time to realize a profit.

But, plainly speaking, both terms refer to the same activity. After all, before you can trade any stock, which involves the process of buying and selling, you need to invest some money in your trading account. In the same way, when you invest in stocks (buying), you also sell them after some time to realize a profit. Hence, investing and trading play the same role.

How stocks trade

You should understand that when you purchase a share of stock, you are not buying it directly from the company. Instead, you are purchasing it from some other shareholder. In the same way, when you sell your stocks, you do not sell them directly to the company. You sell your shares to another investor or investors. Basically, the stock market revolves around the buy and sell process.

There are also loosely regulated places where stocks are bought and sold. These are the over-the-counter exchanges, also known as bulletin boards. However, since these venues are not regulated, buying stocks from these markets is considered risky.

There are always two different ways to set the price of stocks in the market. The most common way is by means of an auction process. Through an auction process, bids and offers to buy and sell are made by buyers and sellers. I beat simply refers to a price at which a person wants to buy a particular stock, while an offer simply refers to the price at which a person wants to sell a stock. When a bid and an offer are matched, then trade is made.

Risks

Before you jump into this venture and start spending real money, you should know the risks involved, so that you will be able to prepare for them and to know if you really want to pursue this kind of investment.

Economic risks

One of the major risks involved when investing in stocks is an economic risk. The problem here is that it is impossible to predict and prevent bad things from happening in the economy. For example, the terrorist attacks in 2001 caused a significant drop in the prices of many stocks in the market. The sudden 9/11 disaster also affected the economy in a negative way.

Market value risk

The market, being composed of people, is hard to predict. Market value risk usually happens when the market starts to ignore your investment and turns to the new investment that is currently gaining popularity. This also takes place when the market collapses.

Company risk

A company is capable of changing. The best company today may no longer be a good company by tomorrow. Unfortunate events may also take place which can dissipate the price of your stocks in the company. This is another reason why you should diversify your investment.

Industrial risk

This is similar to a company risk but affects an entire industry. This, of course, can cause a devaluation of your stocks.

Benefits

If the risks associated with investing in stocks does not destroy your entrepreneurial spirit, then it time for you to find out the benefits involved when you decide to invest in stocks:

Profits

Obviously, investing in stocks can make you earn a decent amount of profit. There is also no ceiling as to how much you can earn. You can buy and sell as many stocks as you want and earn as much as you can.

Tax benefits

In order to encourage investments in stocks, the government usually gives tax benefits to investors.

Make money work for you

Perhaps the main benefit of investing in stocks is that it is a way to make money work for you. If you are able to spot a good company, all you need to do is make an investment, and you can enjoy a continuous amount of profits. This is a good way to make passive income, especially if you are preparing for your retirement or are already in the retirement age.

Ownership

When you purchase common stocks, you become a part-owner of the company. And, since you have stock ownership, you also benefit when the economy grows. This is because growth in the economy translates to income. By investing in the stock market, you also enjoy the benefits that are enjoyed by the business owners.

Stay ahead of inflation

Inflation can be likened to a tax imposed upon all the people. It also adversely affects purchasing power. By investing in stocks, you give yourself a hedge against inflation.

Diversification

As they say, you should not put all your eggs in one basket. Investing in stocks gives you a vast array of options as to where to put your money in.

Dividend income

Some stocks provide dividend income to their owners. This income is released even though the stock concern has already lost its value. Take note, however, that not all stocks are entitled to dividend income.

Is it for you?

It is true that anyone who is of legal age can invest in the stock market. However, it is also true that not anyone can make a profit by investing in stocks. If you are not willing to learn the right strategies and make a thorough and continuous study of the market, then stock investing is not for you. If you cannot be satisfied with a return of 40% on your investment, then this is also not for you. If you have no patience to wait and see what happens to your investment over the course of a few months, then maybe you should look for another investment opportunity. But, if you are the type who is willing to learn and explore new strategies and ideas, if you are willing to put in serious amounts of effort in research and analysis, and if you have enough patience and perseverance, then investing in stocks can be the best thing that you can do, which can change your life for the better.

Where do you get the money to invest?

Many people want to invest in stocks, but the question remains: Where do you get the money to make an investment? Just like any business or investment, investing in stocks also requires a good amount of investment capital. To avoid complications, you should use your own money. Therefore, if you still have not saved up some extra money, then maybe now is the good time to start cutting down your expenses so you can save some money for investing in stocks.

How about OPM? Using OPM or other people's money is also possible, but take note that investing in stocks does not guarantee any profit. In fact, many investors have lost their money in the stock market. Using other people's money by borrowing money is not a recommended method since you run the risk of getting in too much debt, especially if your investment does not work out as you expect. Therefore, the best way is still for you to do your best to save up some money. It does not matter even if it takes you a few months or even a few years just to save up some money for investing. In the meantime, you can use a demo account and come up with a reliable strategy, so that you will be ready when you already have the money that you need to make a real investment in stocks.

Basic terms

When you engage in the stock market, you should know the terms that are commonly used, such as stock symbol, bid and ask price, market price, tick size, and others.

Stock symbol

This is also referred to as stock code. When you look at the stock market, each company a particular code, and this is referred to as stock symbol or stock code. The stock symbol is simply to simplify things so that you do not have to read the whole name of all the corporations. Do not worry; you do not have to memorize the codes. You will be provided a list whenever you make a transaction.

Market price

This simply refers to the price of a stock per share. When the stock market is available for exchanges, the prices of stocks can fluctuate every second, depending on the number of buyers who want make a buy order, as well as those who want to sell.

Bid and ask price

Take note that before a transaction can be completed (buy or sell). Both the buyer and seller must agree upon the price. Of course, buyers want to buy stocks at a low price, while sellers want to be able to sell their stocks as high as possible. The bid and ask price appears on a table and displays the meeting point for both buyers and sellers. There are four things to take note of:

Bid Price – it is the price that a buyer would like to buy a stock.

Bid Size – This refers to the number of shares that a buyer would like to buy at a certain prize.

Ask price – It is the price that a seller wants to sell his stocks.

Ask Size – This refers to the number of shares that a seller would like to sell at a certain prize.

Tick size

This refers to the fluctuation or the smallest change in the price of the stock. Depending on the price range that a particular stock belongs, the tick sizes may also vary. Without using a tick size, buyer and sellers will have a free and huge range of prices to bid and sell.

Board lot

This refers to a summary of tick sizes. You will see how the prices of stocks fluctuate.

Chapter 2
Opening an Account

Before you can get started investing in stocks, you need to open an account with a broker. By simply doing a simple search online you can get a list of different brokers. It is important for you to choose a reliable broker, so that you can get the best services and to ensure safe, reliable, and secure transactions. But, with so many brokers out there that would persuade you to make an investment, how can you tell which one is best suited for your needs best suited for your needs? Here is a set of standards to look for:

Transaction fee

Brokers usually charge a fee for every transaction that you make. In order to save on cost, you should choose a broker that offers a low transaction fee. After all, if you engage in Stock Investing for a long term, you can expect to make many transactions.

Banking

This is an important factor to look into before you make any deposit. It is not unusual to find a broker that offers many methods for making a deposit but only has a limited number of options for making a withdrawal. Make sure that both options for deposit and for withdrawal are available to you.

You should also take note of the documents that you need to submit to your broker before you can make a successful withdrawal. Normally, you will be required to submit some identity documents, such as your driver's license or passport. Make sure that you know the requirements of your broker, and that you have these documents in your possession in order to avoid future problems.

You should also check how many days it will take for your broker to send your money from the time that you request for withdrawal. Normally, your broker should be able to send your money within 1 to 3 banking days. Take note that this is just in the matter of sending your money and not the exact duration on when you will receive your money in your account.

Demo account

Ideally, your broker should offer you a demo account. This account is what you can use to trade and experience the actual stock market without risking any real money. Beginners are strongly recommended to use a demo account. You can also use the demo account to test your strategy, as well as any adjustments that you make.

Minimum deposit requirement

The minimum deposit amount depends on your broker. Some Brokers really require you to deposit a minimum amount of around $100 or even $500 (or higher), while some others do not require any minimum deposit amount.

Maximum withdrawal

If you expect to withdraw a big amount of money in the future, then you should also take note of the maximum withdrawal limit.

This is the maximum amount that you can withdraw, which is usually on a daily basis.

Volume restriction

You should look for a broker that does not have any volume restriction. This means that you should be allowed to buy and sell as many numbers of stocks that you want.

Ratings and reviews

It is also helpful if you check the latest ratings and reviews of your potential broker before you make any deposit. There are many websites online that rate and review different stock brokers. Be sure to read the reviews given by other investors.

Take note of the date of when the last review or rating was given. Also, do not base your decision simply on a single review. It is not uncommon for online brokers to promote themselves by hiring freelance writers to write a positive review about them. The management team and the policy of a broker may also change from time to time. What may be considered as the best online broker today may no longer be a good option by tomorrow. It is also good to keep an eye on new brokers, but you also need to exercise some caution. To be safe, only work with well-established stock brokers.

Mobile feature

These days, most people access the internet through their mobile phones. Your broker should allow you to be able to access your account and buy and sell stocks through your mobile phone. This will allow you to trade anytime and anywhere. Do not worry;

all the well-established brokers have a mobile feature for their platform.

Trading restriction

Your broker should allow you to buy and sell stocks anytime without asking for its permission. This means that you can buy or sell a particular stop without having to call your broker or sending a message to customer support. Simply put, you should be able to trade stocks on your own.

Customer support

It is important that you work with a broker that has a reliable and professional customer support. This will allow you to fix any issues that you may have in the future, especially technical issues. A good way to know if a broker has excellent customer support is by testing it. Before you make any deposit, send a message to customer support and see how well it resolves your inquiry. For example, you can ask the customer support team about the documents that you need to submit when you request for withdrawal. You may also ask for substitute documents in case you do not have the required documents in your possession. Take note of how many days before you get a response, as well as how long it would take them to help you with your inquiry.

Design and layout

Although not necessary, the appearance of the trading platform that you use can also be helpful. It should be professionally designed. It should help set the mood that is best for investing.

Helpful data and features

Your broker should also provide you with data and other information that can help you come up with a sound investment decision. This includes charts and graphs for technical analysis and others. If your broker does not provide you with such data, you might want to use external sites, so that you get the information that you need. Do not worry; reliable brokers always provide such information. They help their investors make the right decisions.

Other charges

There are brokers who charge surcharges. Although surcharges are usually just a small amount, they easily pile up quickly into a significant amount. Some brokers also charge a fee in case of inactivity. This is usually on a monthly basis. This means that you should make even just a single transaction of buying or selling stocks every month. Also, take note of other charges that your broker might impose.

List of brokers

Here is a list of well-established brokers. (Note: Even if you use the brokers on this list, be sure to exercise due diligence. After all, how a broker manages its affairs may change. The best and popular brokers today may no longer be a good choice by tomorrow.)

Charles Schwab

TD Ameritrade

Optionshouse

Scottrade

Merrill Edge

Fidelity Investments

Take note that some banks also offer a service that will allow you to invest in stocks online.

Chapter 3
Strategies

To be successful with investing in stocks, you need to have a strategy. Through the years, different strategies have been developed in order to increase the chances of making a profit in the stock market. You can use any or combine these strategies, but you can also come up with your own. When you engage in the stock market, make sure that you have a winning strategy.

Fundamental analysis

It is worth noting that the value of stocks reflects the performance of a company. Therefore, by understanding the company, you will be more able to understand the behavior of its stocks. When you do fundamental analysis, you focus on the fundamentals of business. This includes reviewing and analyzing a business' financial statements, as well as other things that can reflect its performance.

It is also worth noting the fundamental analysis is not limited to the study of a particular business alone. You should also consider factors that affect the business, such as the economy, government, competition, consumer behavior, and others. After all, the changes in price in the stock market are mere effects of what is happening in the entire market. As you can see, fundamental analysis is very important. Many consider it as the lifeblood of investment for good reasons.

When you read about fundamental analysis or anything that is related to the stock market, you will often encounter the term "fundamentals." People and books on the subject of stock investing will always tell you to focus on the fundamentals. But, what exactly are these fundamentals that you should focus on? Well, the fundamentals refer to the basic, which includes the company's cash flow, conservative gearing, cash flow, financial statements, capital management, and everything that directly relates to the performance of the company.

Technical analysis

If analyzing numbers is not your strong point, and if you are more of a visual person, then you might want to master technical analysis. Technical analysis deals with graphs and charts, which reflect the past and present behavior of the market. By studying the past and present trends, you will be more easily able to predict the future direction of the market. While fundamental analysis is broad in scope, the technical analysis makes things simpler. The theory behind technical analysis is that the different factors that affect the prices of stocks will show up in some form or through price movement. Therefore, by studying and analyzing the movement of the prices of stocks, you will be able to analyze the overall behavior of the stock market. This strategy is also excellent for spotting patterns.

Many people believe that technical analysis is only effective for a short-term investment. But, this is not completely true. Technical analysis can also be the basis of a long-term investment. After all, this approach also includes the examination of the past and present behavior of a particular stock in the market. Therefore, it is in no way limited to just predicting the near-future behavior of the market. However, to use this effectively for a long-term investment, you should keep checking the behavior (movements) of the stock concerned on a regular basis even after you make an investment. This should not be a surprise since this is also what you should do even if you use fundamental analysis or any other strategies. After all, it is a good practice to be on top of all your investments.

Value investing

This is one of the best methods for picking the right stocks. When you use value investing, you look for stocks that have strong fundamentals but are selling at a lower price than their actual value. You should take advantage of this error in valuation.

It is worth noting that when you use value investing, you do not just purchase any stocks that are cheap. Value does not mean cheap or junk. Your objective is to purchase valuable stocks at a bargain.

Growth investing

While value investing focuses on the present moment, Growth Investing focuses on the potential future of business, with little emphasis on the current price of its stocks. Investors who follow this strategy also buy the stocks of a company that trades higher than their actual worth, but this is only made when there is a good belief that the intrinsic worth of the company will soon increase, which will exceed its current valuation.

With this approach, you should look for a company that is growing faster than its competitors. Therefore, the primary focus is on young and start-up companies, since these companies have a big margin for development.

The risk here is that there is no sure strategy that can exactly predict the future valuation of a company. Also, companies may change, and there are many factors that are outside their control.

Income investing

Income investors earn money through dividends as paid by the company. The key here is to choose the companies that have a steady flow of income. Take note that this does not refer to fixed-income securities, but solid dividends. When you use the strategy, it is good to focus on firms and companies that are huge and have already established themselves in the market. This is to ensure that they have a steady flow of dividends.

GARP investing

This strategy is a combination of value investing and growth investing. Media strategy, you need to look for companies that are undervalued but have solid fundamentals and positive growth potential. With this strategy, you are not just concerned with the past and present performance of the company, but you also take into consideration its future direction.

Qualitative analysis

While fundamental analysis is concerned with numbers, qualitative analysis is a more subjective approach. With this strategy, you look for a company that has a strong management, as well as the people who primarily direct the affairs and future of the company. You need to find out who is running the company, such as its CEO, COO, and CFO, among others. You then find out their educational background, as well as their accomplishments and achievements. You should also take into consideration the management philosophy of the company and even the personality of its board of directors. While fundamental analysis places emphasis on the business itself, qualitative analysis puts emphasis on the people who run the business.

Stock mastery

The way to apply this strategy is to choose a stock that you like. What you need to do is to have mastery over that particular stock by learning as much as you can about it on a daily basis. Read everything that you can that has been written on it, especially the latest news and developments. The reason behind this strategy is that the more you know about a particular stock, the easier for you to be able to predict its behavior in the market. You can then take advantage of this "special" knowledge and analysis in the stock market by knowing the perfect time to make a buy and sell order concerning the said stock.

Once you think that you already have expertise over the stock, then you can branch out and master another stock. Just be sure not to let go and forget about the stock that you already know. The key here is to have mastery over as many stocks as possible. Yes, this strategy demands lots of research and analysis, but it can also increase your chances of success significantly.

Feel free to apply as many strategies as you can, such as fundamental analysis, technical analysis, and others. The important thing is for you to have a better understanding of the behavior of your chosen stock. The more strategies or approaches that you apply, the better. Also, do an in-depth research about your chosen stock, and try to find out information that the ordinary public does not know about it.

Conservative

You should follow a conservative approach, especially if you are a beginner. With a conservative approach, you do not change the amount of your investment. Therefore, the way to profit is to increase your rate of success. Generally, when you follow this approach, you should only spend around 1 to 2 percent of your total funds per trade. Instead of making one big investment on a particular trade, you diversify your position. By doing so, you are also able to minimize your risk.

Progressive

This is an aggressive form of strategy where you increase the amount that you invest each time you suffer a loss. The key here is that by increasing your investment, you can also increase your profit potential. By doing so, you can recover your past losses and even earn some positive profits. Just be careful when you use this strategy because this tends to exhaust your funds quickly.

Mixed

With this strategy, you combine all the other strategies that you know. The principle behind this strategy is that since the stock market keeps on changing, then it is only logical to say that you should also keep on changing your strategy. Therefore, you can use fundamental analysis for one particular trade, and then you can use qualitative analysis for another, value investing for another, and so on. The key here is to keep on shuffling the strategies as you keep on investing in different kinds of stocks.

Develop your own

With so many strategies out there, there is still no strategy that can guarantee the direction of the stock market. The best way to still for you to develop your own strategy. You do not always have to come up with a completely unique strategy. You can simply make some adjustments with the strategies that you already know. Always remember that the stock market keeps on changing just as people and businesses keep on developing. Therefore, you should always work on your strategy.

Sources of facts

When you read any book that teaches you how to invest in stocks, they will always suggest that you focus on the facts and make an analysis. But, how do you get these facts? Is making a search online good enough?

Company's annual report

Companies release an annual report on a regular basis. Such report will tell you key information about the company, such as their financial data. This is important, especially when doing fundamental analysis. So, be sure to get your hands on this report.

Analysts' report

This is the report made by analysts and research departments. You can find a good number of these reports online. This includes detailed commentaries and solid data, which can help you come up with a sound investment decision. This can also be provided by your broker.

Form 10-K

This is a comprehensive financial data and is required to be filed yearly with the SEC. This usually involves the company's balance sheet for two years, a history of its stock price for five years, as well as its earnings and dividends.

Value line investment survey

This is a huge collection of data, which includes the prices, dividends, earnings, and other records of a company for many years. You can find this by visiting libraries.

Expert comments

You can find many expert comments online, usually made by people who are real experts and those who claim to be experts. Therefore, be careful about the information that you get from these comments. You can easily find these details by doing a search online. Mostly, websites that are about the stock market have articles that share the views and pieces of advice from "experts."

What to look for in a company

With so many companies out there offering their stocks out to the public, how do you know the ones that are a good investment? Although there is a hard and fast rule on what guarantees a good investment, there are signs that you can look for to increase your chances of making a profit.

Per-share earning

Look for companies whose shares have a stable earning growth. Also, look for those who have the practice of reinvesting a part of their earnings in order to help the business expand or grow. You can also compare the per-share earnings with a number of the dividends that have been paid out to stockholders.

Price-earnings ratio

The price-earnings ratio or P/E is considered by some experts as the most important thing to consider before buying a stock. This simply refers to the price of a share after you divide it by the company's per-share earnings. For example, if a company sells its stock for $30 and the company has earned $3 for the previous 12-month period, then the P/E ratio of the stock is 10. The P/E ratio shows just how much money the investors are willing to spend for every dollar that the company earns. This is a significant basis. As such, it is usually listed in newspapers.

When you check the P/E of a company, you should compare it with the P/E of other similar companies. There is also no quick rule to determine the right level of P/E of a company. The problem with having a high P/E is that if the company's earnings disappoint its investors, then the price of its stocks can experience a significant decrease in price. Consequently, a very low P/E is usually frowned upon by investors since it signals it that the company is not capable of rapid growth.

A way to use P/E ratios to determine stocks that have a potential to earn you profit is by finding companies that have low P/E relative to other companies included in the same industry. Assuming that the company also shows positive signs of strengths, then it may be a good investment. But, making an investment decision simply based on a low P/E is also not 100% that it is a profitable investment, because a low P/E may also be the result when investors simply do not trust the company to be able to do well on its earnings. Therefore, picking a stock based on the price-earning ratio alone is not a recommended method. But, you can use it as a secondary basis for your investment decision.

Take note that the basis here is only the P/E trail for the past 12 months. There is no assurance of any positive P/E for the future. And, you only earn a profit when the price of the stock that you buy today increases in the future. Therefore, also take note of the future estimates.

Return on equity

Look for companies that display a consistently high return on equity. Such return must be compared with companies that belong to the same industry. If you find a company that has a consistent return on equity of at least 15% is a good sign.

A company's return on equity refers to the company's net profit after deducting the taxes and dividing by its book value. It demonstrates the company's earning in the business. If the return on equity grows year after year, then it is a good sign that it may be a profitable investment. But, if the behavior of the company's return on equity is staggering, declining, or is erratic, then it may be due to problems with the company's debt and profit margins. In such case, you should stay away from such company.

Debt-equity ratio

Compare the debts of a company with its shareholder's equity. As a rule, a company with a debt that exceeds 35% of its shareholder's equity is a bad choice. You can check the company's annual reports to find information regarding its debt.

Popularity

Pay attention to how much interest and popularity the company is gaining. As a rule, a company that is able to draw a steady flow of positive attention gets one step ahead of the competition. The prices of its stocks can be expected to move upward. However, this popularity must be backed up with solid promotions, and there must be a continuous effort to make the company more popular.

Industry leader

A company that becomes a leader in the industry or has a big potential to be a leader in its industry is usually a good investment because such company enjoys several advantages and gains the trust of the market. For example, instead of merely following the price set in the market, an industry leader can assume its own price, and all other companies in the industry are running the same business merely follows what the industry leader dictates. Since the company is a leader in the industry, it also has a more established presence in the market. It can also afford to present new products since the market is more acceptable if the products come from a leader in the industry.

Research and development

Although not a major factor, it is still good advice to invest in a company that makes its own investment in research and development. This is a god sign that the company is committed to developing itself, which usually translates to an increase in the value of its stocks. Now, many companies have a research and development sector. What you can do here is to compare their spending on this sector to be able to know which of them is more committed to development. Of course, having a lower investment in research and development does not prove that the company is less focused on developing itself, but a company that has a high investment in research and development, especially if such investment was made just recently, often leads to an increase in the value of its stocks.

Chapter 4
Best Practices

In order to increase the probability of making a profit, you can also apply the best practices observed by successful stock investors. Although these practices do not guarantee a favorable outcome, they remain as the key cornerstones of real and continues success.

Start small

It does not matter whether you have a big amount in your account that you can use for investing in stocks. When you are a beginner, you should start small. For a start, your objective is to get comfortable with the system and familiarize yourself with the real market. This is also the best moment for you to test the water and see if this is something that you want to pursue. As a rule, you should invest not more than 5% of your total funds for every order that you make. The keys for you to focus on increasing your rate of success. This means that you should make more good investments decisions than decisions that cause you to lose money. This approach will also help you to minimize your losses. After all, beginners tend to commit so many blunders. Therefore, start small or, if you want, just use the demo account until you reach a point where you already have a reliable strategy.

Research

If there is one thing shared by all successful investors in stocks, it is the continuous habit of researching and analyzing the stock market. This, of course, is not limited to the stocks themselves, but also considers the factors which affect the fluctuations of the prices in the stock market, such as the latest news, businesses, consumer behavior, and even the government, among others.

Continuous research is a habit that should be the cornerstone of your strategy. After all, the behavior of the stock market is not something that is made randomly. If you know the right factors to consider and examine them properly, you can increase your chances of success by more than 70%.

Be updated on the news

The news reveals important information about the stock market, especially reports about the government, businesses, technology, and others. To some extent, the news can give you an idea of what stocks would be a profitable investment. The news will also reveal to you the status of the economy. Of course, when the economy is doing good, prices of stocks tend to increase. However, when the economy is going bad, then you should be cautious about making any buy order.

Money management

Some investors do not lose their money because of choosing the wrong investments. Mismanagement of your account is also an effective and quick way to go bankrupt. Therefore, make sure that you have a good and stable plan on how to manage your money.

Good money management includes a solid plan on how much you are willing to invest, as well as how much you want to invest each time you make a buy order. Accordingly, you should also have a plan on how long you are going to hold on to a particular stock before selling it. You need to strike a balance between your investment and the profits that you can make out of them. Needless to say, you should also consider your expenses.

Writing an investment journal

Having an investment journal is not a requirement. However, keeping a journal can also be useful. It will allow you to see yourself as an investor from a different perspective, which would allow you to think outside the box and come up with a better strategy or decision.

Do not worry; you do not have to be a professional writer just to come up with a journal. All you need is to be completely honest with everything that you record in your journal and to update your journal on a regular basis. Your journal should be like a mirror that reflects your state as an investor.

You can write anything that you want in your journal as long as it is related to being an investor in stocks. Ideally, your journal should also include the reasons why you want to invest in stocks, as well as your main objectives and goals. Your journal should also include the strategies that you have, as well as new learning that you encounter along the way. You can also record the mistakes that you commit so that you can avoid them more easily in the future.

From time to time, make it habit to read your journal and make reflections. If you do, you will be surprised as to how much your journal can teach you about yourself and how you can further develop your investment strategy.

Patience

Successful investors are patient. They pick the right stocks and exercise patience. The wait for weeks and even months for the price of their stocks to increase. Only then will they make a sell order and enjoy a good amount of profit. But, of course, patience should not be exercised blindly. This means that you should hold on to good and profitable stocks and let go of those stocks whose price is continuously falling down.

Diversify

As they say, do not put all your eggs in one basket. In the same way, when you trade stocks, you can minimize your losses by diversifying your investment. Placing all your money in *one* *i*nvestment is too risky. After all, no matter how much research and Analysis you make, there is no guarantee that a certain investment will earn you any profit. There is always the risk of losing your investment. You can diversify by making multiple trades instead of just a single transaction. Of course, when you diversify, good money management is also needed.

Take advantage of trends

Trends or patterns appear from time to time. Even a random generator creates patterns. When you notice a particular pattern in the stock market, you should take advantage of it immediately. You should be able to place a corresponding buy or sell order before the trend disappears.

Focus on the numbers

No matter what the media promotes or what is being promoted online, the only thing that matters is the numbers that appear. After all, the stock market remains to be a numbers game. Therefore, focus on the numbers. This also means being objective and logical in your approach.

Take a break

Some people think that investing in stocks is easy because you can do it in the comfort of your home. Well, successful stock investors know better. They know that to have continuous success, you need to put in serious efforts. And, making a significant amount of money usually takes time. Therefore, allow yourself to relax and take a break from time to time. A good way to relax is to do something that is completely not related to the business of investing in stocks. This is also a good way to remove stress. Once you regain a clear mind and a relaxed body, you can go back to your investments, and you will be able to make better investment decisions. Also, being too caught up with work tends to make you over-analyze things, which is not good. Take a note that this does not mean that you can be lazy. You should take a break because you need it, because you deserve it, and not because you do not feel like working.

Develop your strategy

Just as the stock market continues to change and evolve, you should continue to work on your strategy. It is worth noting that developing a strategy is a lifelong journey. You must keep yourself updated with the latest developments, and your strategy should be flexible enough to adapt to changes. As you may already know, there is no such thing as a permanent strategy. Just ask businesses and the consumer market continue to grow, your strategy must also develop and match up with the changing time.

Learn from your mistakes

Always learn from your mistakes. When you engage in the stock market, committing mistakes is normal. In fact, mistakes are inevitable. They are part of the game. Even the best investors in the world are also prone to committing mistakes. But, you should always learn from every mistake that you make, so that you can avoid committing the same or similar mistake in the future. It is disappointing when you lose an investment. Learn not to be disheartened. Be kind to yourself and move on. But you learning from your mistakes, you can use them as stepping stones that can turn you into a better investor.

Have a stop-loss limit

A stop-loss limit is a limit that you set by which you will stop holding on to a losing stock. This will help prevent you from losing all your investment. Ideally, you should already set a stop-loss limit even before you place a buy order. For example, if you set a stop-loss limit at 20%, this means that you can hold on even to a losing stock provided its price does not drop by more than 20%. But, once its price drops by more than 20%, then you should make a sell order immediately. You should then accept whatever losses that you may have had, and start a new transaction, in case you see an opportunity to make a profit.

Proper timing

Just like in anything, proper timing is also important when you invest in stocks. Having a good understanding as to when to make a buy order and a sell order is crucial to success. Some investors also commit the mistake of researching too much that by the time they make an actual investment, the opportunity to earn a profit has already lapsed. There are others who continue to buy particular stocks without realizing that their price is already about to drop, just like in the case of a pump and dump scheme. Observing proper timing is important both for buying and selling stocks.

Only invest the money that you can afford to lose

This is a common advice given to gamblers. The same advice applies to those who want to invest in the stock market. Only invest the money that you can afford to lose. Although there is no assurance that you will lose your money and that there is even a chance for you to make a profit, you should not use "important" money when you invest in stocks. Therefore, do not use the money that you need to cover your responsibilities and everyday necessities. After all, no extent of research and analysis can guarantee a return of positive profits.

It is also not right to use your savings. If you want to save money for investment, you should have a different account for your savings, and another account for the money that you can use for investing. Most people use their savings for their investments. This is a wrong approach since you run the risk of losing all your savings.

Lower your risks

An effective way to minimize your losses is to lower your risk. After all, your total losses cannot exceed the total risk. There are some things that you can do that can minimize your risks, such as choosing a reliable broker to work with. You should choose a well-established broker so that you do not have to worry about your broker suddenly disappearing with all your investment money and profits. Another effective way to lower your risk is to ensure that every investment decision that you make is backed up by sufficient research and deep analysis. Take note that the more you lower your risks, the more you can cut down your losses. Of course, you cannot completely remove all the risks of an investment, but by minimizing the risks, you also increase your chances of success.

Limit your orders

By limiting your order, you can avoid overpaying. Use a limit order to set an order to limit the maximum and minimum amount that you are willing to buy or sell a particular stock. This guarantees that any transaction that you enter into will be at your preferred price, or better.

There are three kinds of orders that you should look into: a market order, stop order, and limit order. A market order is simply an order to buy at a price that is considered the best market price. Take note that the basis here is the market price and not your preferred price. A limit order will allow you to set your preferred price, and this order can be filled in should another person agree on the price. A stop order is a limitation that you place as to how much you are willing to pay for stocks.

Cash out

Some investors do not like cashing out with an aim to grow their investment money or funds. Take note that although building a bigger investment money is a good part of a strategy, it does not mean that you should not cash out any of your profits. After all, profits are only completely realized once you convert them into real cash. But, without cashing out, if your profits only remain on the screen or the trading platform, then they are only as good as the money in your demo account, which means that they are worth nothing. Therefore, learn to cash out from time to time so you can truly enjoy your earnings.

You do not have to withdraw all your money or all your profits at once. If you want, you can just set a particular rate, for example, cashing out 25% of your weekly earnings. It is important for you to withdraw your money. Also, by withdrawing your money, it automatically minimizes your potential losses.

Act only when there is gain

Successful investors know that every action in the whole scheme of investment matters. A simple mistake in making decisions can cause a serious loss. Therefore, you should only take action when there is a good probability of earning a profit. Other things, especially if there is no or little probability of making any profit, it would be better for you to be inactive and not make any decision. As already mentioned, proper timing is essential to success. Take note that just because you have funds available in your account does not mean that you should place any kind of order, whether a buy order or a sell order. Learn to just observe, but be sure to act quickly when you notice an opportunity to profit.

Be professional

The way you approach investing in stocks is important. If you intend to take stocks investing seriously, then you should approach it professionally. This means that you should consider it as you would a business. Treating it professionally also means that you should give it the time that it needs.

Time management

Most people who invest in the stock market are not full-time investors. Many of them have day jobs and other responsibilities. With such hectic schedule, how are you able to manage your time properly? The key here is to invest less. However, this does not mean that you will give it less focus. You invest less because you also get to give it less time. After all, every single investment that you make should be supported by solid research and analysis.

Hence, if you only have a limited time that you can devote with investing, then also lower the number of your investments. If you want, you can simply increase the amount of your investment to compensate for the limited number of transactions that you make.

Get as much information as you can

The key to success with stock investing heavily depends upon the information that you have. Therefore, strive to get as much information as you can. The more you know about a particular company, the more you can tell if it is a good investment or not. However, it is also important for you to realize that you should not get caught up with too much information. Choose only the information that will help you with a particular trade. After all, there is no end as to the information that you can get regarding a particular stock.

Continuous development

Always aim for continuous development. Even if you have made 10 consecutive profitable investments, it does not mean that you can be over confident already of your strategy. The stock market can have drastic changes, so you should always be on guard. Always strive for continuous improvement and keep working on your strategy.

Take advantage of the pump and dump

You can take advantage of the pump and dump scheme by riding it during the time that it is favorable for an investor. Take note that in a pump and dump scheme, the price of a particular stock tends to increase as the stock is being hyped or promoted. This is your opportunity to profit. By buying the stock and selling it just before its price begins to decline, you get to take advantage of the situation. You can turn what otherwise would be a fraudulent and negative circumstance into a goldmine. By knowing when to get in and having the discipline to escape the scheme (sell) just before the price drops, you get to earn a profit and is able to take advantage of the efforts of the one who runs such fraudulent scheme.

Take note of stock split

When a company declares a stock split, it is usually a good sign. It means that the value of its stocks has increased so high that they need to split the stocks so that their value will be lower. This is because there are investors who do not like to invest in stocks that already have a high price. For example: If you own 50 stocks worth $50 per stock and a stock split is declared, then you will end up with 100 stocks worth $25 per stock. As you can see, it is still the same since the amount per stock is also split in half. Take note that a stock split is not always in half. The stock can be divided into three, or even more. This all depends upon the declaration of the board of directors of the company.

In case of a legitimate stock split, then it is an opportunity for you to buy good-quality stocks. Since the split is declared as a result of the positive performance of the business, there is a high chance that such performance will continue, which will make the value of the stocks after the split to increase as well.

There is, however, a situation that you should avoid, and that is the reverse split. As the name suggests, the reverse split is simply a stock split in reverse. For example, if you have 100 shares at $10 per share and a reverse split is done, then you will have 50 shares at $20 per share. As you can see, the price of the stocks increases significantly. Now, although this may look good, it is actually a bad signal. It is, in fact, a fraudulent scheme resorted to by a struggling company. By doing a reverse split, it aims to make it appear to investors that the company is doing really well. This is to persuade investors to make an investment in the company, which the latter (company) will use to save itself from bankruptcy. Of course, a reverse split does not always mean that the company will no longer be able to gain stability. However, it is still not a good sign. Therefore, instead of investing in such company, which necessarily involves a high risk, you would do better by investing in another company that is actually doing well.

Buy low, sell high

The old saying of buying low and selling high also applies in the stock market. The important thing is to be able to determine which of the many stocks you should buy, and when you should sell them while observing proper timing at the same time.

You also have to deal with stock volatility, which is caused by many factors and movements of stocks in the stock market. But, how do you know when you are really buying low? There are things that you should consider, such as the past trend of the prices of a particular stock, as well as the prices of stocks of those that belong to the same industry and engaged in a similar business. After all, the strength of one company is only relative to the strength of other companies that belong to the same industry.

Of course, you only buy a stock if you believe that the value of its stocks will soon increase. We have already discussed the signs to look for before buying a stock, but how do you know when to sell a stock?

Of course, the simple answer is simply to sell a stock once you have realized a profit. The exception here is selling a losing stock in order to avoid incurring more losses. After all, chasing after your losses is not a recommended approach when investing in stocks. Now, before you sell your stocks, here are some things that you should take note of:

Change in a company's fundamentals

When you notice that the fundamentals of the company begin to weaken, then it is time to reconsider your investment. Now, a small decline in a company's fundamentals does not necessarily mean that you should sell out your stocks right away. You need to closely examine the company. Take note of its latest financial statements, if available, and pay attention to how it performs in the market with regard to its competitors. In case that you still cannot decide despite examining the company's records, a better option for you to do is to sell your stocks.

Cutting of dividends

If the company begins to cut down its dividends, it is usually a sign that the company may be in trouble. After all, it would not cut down the earnings distributed to its stockholders if it is doing well.

When profit is already realized

The safest way to make a sell order is when you have already realized a profit. After all, many investors do not just lose money simply because of choosing the wrong stocks. Sometimes, they lose their money when they hold on to the right stocks for a long period. You should not underestimate the volatility of the stock market. Therefore, do not hesitate to make a sell order once you have achieved your target profit.

Chapter 5

Common Mistakes and How to Avoid Them

You can increase your chances of success and minimize your losses by knowing the common mistakes that beginners and even intermediate stock investors make. It is important for you to be aware of these pitfalls so that you can make the necessary adjustments and be able to avoid them.

It is worth noting that some of these pitfalls are difficult to avoid. In fact, you may still commit them even though you are aware of them. Should you fall into these pitfalls for any reason, do not be hard on yourself. Instead, learn from your mistakes and try to do better.

Insufficient research

If you want to be successful in trading stocks, you should spend serious time doing research. It is the amount and quality of your research that will put you ahead of the competition and the stock market. Unfortunately, many investment decisions are made based on insufficient data or poor research. But comma what is the right amount of research? The answer to this question varies because the amount of research that you need for an investment depends on several circumstances. Of course, you must study the factors that directly affect your investment. The important thing is for you to be honestly satisfied and confident of your investment decision.

If there is one thing that separates investing in stocks from gambling, it is the presence of factors that you can study in order to better determine the behavior of the stock market. Take note that the prices of the different stocks in the market are not created by a mere random generator. Rather, such changes are caused by the actions of real people and businesses. In fact, the changes in the prices of the different stocks are very logical if only you know how to determine the right factors, as well as how to examine them properly.

It is important for you to remember not to make any decision that is based on insufficient research. Of course, sometimes, even a decision based on poor research can still bring in some profits; however, you cannot expect to make money out of it in the long run. This is because anything that comes from an insufficient research is only as good as gambling or relying on mere luck.

Relying on expert advice

When you are a beginner, it is helpful to read that tips and comments made by the experts. However, once you learn more about the stock market, you should no longer rely on expert advice video. These days, it is very easy to promote something we just a few clicks of a mouse. Unfortunately, many of these experts online are not real experts. In fact, you should not be surprised if they have more losses than profits. Therefore, I do not believe everything that you read online. Always take every information that you receive with a grain of salt.

It is also noteworthy that even the real experts also commit mistakes from time to time. This is because the stock market is not easy to predict. In fact, sometimes, you can say that the stock market is unpredictable. Therefore, it is very important for you to develop your own understanding of the stock market. After all, if there is any difference between the experts and the beginners, it is the fact that experts have their own way of viewing the market, and are able to support their views with good and logical reasons. Of course, this does not mean that you should avoid reading what other people say, even those who promote themselves as experts. After all, there is always something that you can learn from anything. A good approach is for you to compare your own view with the view of the so-called experts, but never have the habit of relying on expert advice completely without thinking. Not to mention, some of these so-called experts also participate in fraudulent schemes, such as the pump and dump scheme.

Applying an untested strategy

When investing in stocks, having a reliable strategy is important. Without a good strategy, you cannot expect to me so much profit with the stock market. In fact, considering how the stock market is designed, you can even lose all your investment money. Therefore, always use a strategy, and be sure to test your strategy before you apply it. A good way to test your strategy is by taking advantage of a demo account where you can participate in a live market without risking any real money.

A common mistake made by so many investors is not testing their strategy after making some adjustments. Since the stock market is alive and moving, your strategy will also change from time to time. Remember that when you change anything in your strategy, even if it is just a slight adjustment, you should test it again several times to be able to gauge its effectiveness. After all, even a minor change in one's strategy can create a big impact on his investment.

Chasing after your losses

You should not chase after your losses. When you do, there is a higher probability for you to lose all your money. Yes, by chasing after your loss yes, you may be able to recover your money and even bring some profits along the way. However, in the long run, there is a very high probability for you to lose everything. Although not chasing after one's losses is common advice, so many stock investors still commit the same mistake. For you to avoid this, you need to understand what chasing one's losses really means. Normally, you chase after your losses by increasing the amount of your wager or investment in order to recover your previous losses. By doing so, you risk a larger amount of money. This increased risk is what can cause you to lose all your investment money. Take note that when you increase the amount of your investment, your entire portfolio or bankroll may suffer. This usually changes your strategy into an aggressive one, and the total funds in your account may not be ready for such kind of strategy. Also, chasing after your losses tends to make you trade under pressure, which may prevent you from making a sound investment decision. Instead of chasing after your losses, you should accept any losses and just focus on developing your investment strategy to earn more profits.

Trading under pressure

Never trade under any form of undue pressure. Trading under pressure can cloud your judgment, and it usually leads to severe consequences. Therefore, do not use as an investment money the money that you need to cover for your household bills and other obligations. Trading under pressure also arises after you experience a serious loss. If this happens to you, just relax and take a break for a while.

Being too aggressive

Especially if you are a beginner, being too aggressive is not a good strategy. Indeed, by increasing the amount of your investment, you can increase your potential profit. However, you should also consider that by increasing the amount of your investment, you also increase your risk. When you are a beginner, you should focus on increasing your rate of success instead of the amount of profit that you can get. After all, once you develop a reliable strategy, you can confidently increase the amount of your investment.

Sentimentality

Some investors fall in love with a particular stock and decide to hold on to it no matter what. They hope that by remaining loyal to such stock, they can one day build their empire. You should keep in mind that sentimentality does not apply when you deal with the stock market. After all, the stock that you like so much and even the whole stock market do not care about you and your feelings. Therefore, do not be sentimental. Be open and flexible to changes

— because they are a natural part of the stock market. Feel free to switch to another stock when your current stocks are already showing signs that their price is about to hit the ceiling and start going down.

Forcing a pattern

When you use technical analysis and analyze graphs and charts, you should not force yourself to see any pattern. Unfortunately, many beginners commit the mistake of thinking that there is always a pattern to be recognized. Take note that patterns come and go. Also, before a pattern can be established, a certain trend must repeat itself at least twice. It is also worth noting that even though a certain trend has repeated itself twice or thrice, it does not automatically mean that it will be repeated again. Therefore, I better practice to follow is to study the market and use the pattern as a secondary basis for your investment.

Being a victim of the pump and dump scheme

The pump and dump scheme is a fraudulent technique used by unscrupulous investors. In a pump and dump scheme, a person promotes a certain stock and spreads good rumors about it. When this happens, it draws the attention of so many people. When this happens, the value of the stock that is being promoted increases. The owner of the stock then sells his stock at a premium price. Many investors then by the stocks thinking that they are a good investment. However, what happens here is that after buying the stocks, the promotion also stops. As a result, the value of the said stocks will begin to decrease significantly. As a natural consequence, the seller of the stocks makes a good profit while the buyer suffers a loss.

This is another reason why you should develop your own understanding of the stock market. It is easy to fall for a pump and dump scheme when you do not have your own understanding of how it and the market work.

Copying other people's investment decisions

There are platforms this day's that will allow you to copy the Investments made by other people. Usually, those who know little about stocks merely duplicate the Investments made by the so-called experts. This is another mistake because it is hard to determine who the real experts are. And, even the best stock investors still commit mistakes from time to time. A better approach is for you to compare your own strategy with the decisions of the so-called experts. From there, you can develop your strategy and make it better.

Using the same losing strategy

Some investors mistakenly think that because a certain strategy has lost already a number of times would mean that it is about to make a profit already. They think that the stock market follows fair odds, that sometimes you will lose and other times you will win. But, this is not correct. The stock market does not give any attention to any odds of winning or losing, and a single trade is totally independent of other trades or transactions that you make. You also cannot expect the stock market to balance out your right and wrong decisions. Of course, even the best strategy in the world will still lose from time to time. But, if a particular strategy that you use has already lost consecutively, then perhaps it would be better for you to take a break for a while, develop your strategy, make some changes, and try again some other time. Also, do not forget to test your strategy several times before using it.

Regular practice

You cannot be good at investing in stocks just by reading. Reading or even memorizing all the books that have been reading about stocks and the stock market will not make you the best investor in the world. True knowledge of the stock market requires actual experience and continuous practice. Keep on practicing and do not rush the process of learning.

Chapter 6
Take the Leap

Now that you have the right knowledge of investing in the stock market, it is time for you to take the actual steps and start your journey. The following will guide you on the actual steps that you should do to get started. The goal here is to get your feet wet, so the focus will be on getting you on your journey to stock investing.

Get committed to your goal

The first step is for you to set a commitment. Although this advice may already be considered a cliché, having a commitment is an important part of your journey as a stock investor. At this moment, it does not matter whether you are successful or not, whether you are poor or rich, or whatever it may be that you are coming form, the only thing that matters is where you are heading. This time you will work on your financial life and attain financial freedom by investing in stocks.

Take a moment to write down your investing goal or goals, as well as how important they are to your life. Read whatever you have written aloud and commit to it.

Create an investment account

Creating an account has been discussed in chapter 2 of this book. By now, you should already have a broker in mind where you will open an account. Do not worry; opening an account is easy and free. It only takes less than five minutes to register and open your investment account. Also, if the broker offers a mobile feature (which it should), be sure to have it downloaded or bookmarked on your mobile phone for easy access and convenience.

Use the demo account

Spend some time with the demo account. Apply your strategy and give it some time. Be sure to monitor your progress for a few days. Once you are satisfied with your strategy, and if you think that you are confident enough for the real thing, then it is time for you to make our first deposit.

Make a deposit

It is time for you to place a deposit. The amount of deposit depends on the required minimum deposit as set by your chosen broker, as well as your preferred amount. One you have decided upon the amount that you are willing to invest, then it is time for you to get it into your account by following the instructions posted on your broker's website. If you have any questions, feel free to contact customer support.

Apply your strategy

It is now time for you to apply your strategy and make a buy order to get your first stocks. Be sure that you have done all the necessary research and analysis in order to increase your chances of success.

Monitor

Monitor your investment for the next days or weeks or even months. Be sure to make a sell order immediately if the price of your stocks reaches your stop-loss limit. In the same way, if the price of your stocks reaches your desired rate, do not hesitate to make a sell order. Remember that your objective is to stay in the game and have a high rate of success. Make a sell order while you are still on the winning edge.

Continue

Now, simply continue your journey, persevere, and strive to be a better investor. Be sure to back up every investment decision that you make with sufficient research and analysis. The more information that you know about particular stocks, the more you can predict their behavior. If your first investment experiences a profit, then all well and good for you; but if not, then just take the loss as a cost of learning. Continue to do your best and learn more.

Chapter 7
Other Matters

When you invest in stocks, you will soon find (and even be tempted) to invest in other things, such as penny stocks and even binary options. Although there is nothing wrong with investing in these things, you should exercise more caution in doing so.

Many people who invest in the stock market get tempted to invest in penny stocks and binary options because such kind of investment offers a handsome return within a short period of time.

So, just an overview, a penny stock is any stock that has a price of less than $5. It is still a stock of a company. The thing about penny stocks is that they are highly speculative. Their prices fluctuate heavily.

Now, about binary options, when you invest in binary options, you only have to predict whether the price of an underlying asset will increase or decrease at expiry time, which can be as fast as 30 seconds. If you make the correct prediction, then you can earn about 80%-90% net profit. This is as close to casino gambling as you can get. But, what is the catch? Well, in case you make the wrong prediction, then you lose the whole amount that you invested for that particular trade.

High risk, high return

As you can see, the attractive return of investing in penny stocks and binary options is counterbalanced by the high risk involved in this kind of investment.

How about day trading?

Day trading also applies when you invest in stocks. This only means that you should limit the duration of all your investments in one day. So, you open your positions in the morning and close them out in the evening. You then start the process all over again with a clean slate the next trading day. You can adapt this kind of approach if you want, especially if your investment for the day experiences an increase in price (profit). However, this is not as easy as it looks. It is not uncommon to find traders and investors who wait for weeks, and even months, just to get a significant profit.

Diversify

If you want, you can diversify your investment by placing some of your investments in penny stocks and binary options. Take note, however, that penny stocks are different from common stocks. Penny stocks tend to be more volatile and riskier. You also cannot expect to receive any dividends from the company. As with binary options, it is simply very risky. Be very careful.

Financial freedom

People who invest in stocks usually look for financial freedom. With practice, serious efforts and luck, this is doable. However, you should keep in mind that the amount of your gain when investing in stocks is a percentage of your investment. Therefore, to have significant profits, you need to make a significant amount of investment.

This book does not promote any kind of hype. It deals with the reality of investing in stocks in as honest and practical manner as possible. When you invest in stocks, a 50% increase in your investment per year is already considered high. Therefore, be realistic if financial freedom is your purpose. This means that you should also invest a big amount of money. You can, however, start small and make it grow through the years.

The best way is for you start early and reinvest your dividends, so you can come up with a big portfolio. By investing, you let your money do the work for you. The key lies in choosing the right investment options to place your money in. By now, you already have an idea of how to choose good stocks to invest in. making money with stocks is not easy, just as it is also not easy to make money with other kinds of investment. But, with hard work, due diligence, patience, and practice, financial freedom is within your reach.

Taxes

You should check the applicable tax laws in your country, so you will know the taxes that you need to pay. Normally, you will get taxed every time you sell an investment at a profit. Take note that there can be different tax applications for a short-term investment and a long-term investment. For a long-term investment, a lower tax rate is usually imposed. In the U.S., the tax rate for a short investment can be as high as 35%, while only 15% is imposed for a long-term investment. Also, be sure to claim any tax benefits that may be available. You also need to pay taxes on the dividends that you receive. When it comes to managing your taxes, it is best to consult with a lawyer, so you will know your tax liabilities, as well as any tax benefits that you may claim.

Seven qualities of a successful stock investor

1. Hardworking

Every successful investor knows the importance of hard work. While other people think that investing in stocks simply means looking at a few charts and reading the latest news, a successful investor spends hours doing in-depth research and serious analysis before making an investment.

2. Proactive

A successful investor always finds ways to learn more. He is not satisfied simply from what he read on the Internet or what he reads from books. He tries to discover as much as he can about the subject. By doing so, he is able to learn more than the ordinary man, and this allows him to draw better conclusions and make better investment decisions.

3. Patient

Every successful investor knows the importance of patience. He knows that it is a virtue that he should always observe. He is patient enough to spend weeks and even months to wait out a bad streak, and then he enjoys the flow of income which is a fruit of his patience. Of course, he also has the ability to completely let go of stock if he realizes that holding on will only cause him to lose more in the long run.

4. Strategic

A successful investor will never commence any kind of trade without a reliable strategy. He spends hours and even sleepless nights in developing his strategy. In the process, he has to let go of strategies that he has developed for hours if he sees that they are not good enough, and then he holds on and continues to work on those that he believes can increase his chances of success.

5. Honest

A successful trader is honest with himself. He accepts whenever he faces a loss, and remains humble during times of victory, knowing that he still has much to learn. By being honest with himself, he is more able to come up with good strategies, since he is able to spot his weaknesses easily.

6. Disciplined

A successful investor is well disciplined. He sticks to the strategy that he has worked on for hours and does not allow himself to get directed by his emotions. This is important, especially when one deals with the stock market since the market does not care about its investors. This sense of discipline is also present in his day-to-day activities as he keeps himself updated on the news and continues his research and analysis of the market. He is disciplined not only in making money but also in cutting down his losses. Also, he disciplines himself enough to exercise a good amount and continuous focus on his investment, making sure that he is on top of all his investments, and treats his work (investing in stocks) as a major priority.

7. Faithful

Every successful investor is faithful. He is faithful without being arrogant. He believes in himself, and more importantly, in God. He knows that he can achieve his goals no matter how difficult they may be. And, during times of both success and defeat, he prays to God and remains kind and courageous.

Conclusion

Thanks for making it through to the end of this book. We hope it was informative and able to provide you with all of the tools you need to achieve your goals whatever they may be.

The next step is to apply everything that you have learned. So, open an account today, start investing, and make some money!